OUR FIENDS HAVE COME TO VISIT US

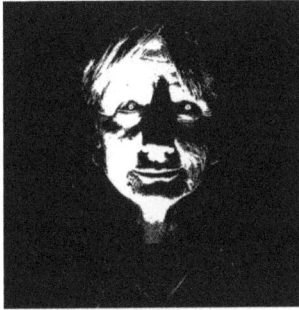

by

James Louis Carcioppolo

JamesLouisCarcioppolo

Lost Sonnet Publishing
Livermore, CA 94550

ISBN: 978-0-9858444-4-8

Book design and text
James L. Carcioppolo

Our fiends have come to visit us:

Rolleen and Jim, Clyde and Gus.

And many more

Who crave gore.

How they love to make a fuss!

*(any resemblance to persons or places
is strictly coincidental)*

CONTENTS

ABEL ANDREWS

There, beneath a pile of rocks,
Without his shirt, without his socks,

Abel Andrews woke up dead
With a hatchet in his head.

As light was leaking from the day
He slowly pushed the rocks away;

And since his waking was delayed,
He found his body quite decayed.

So bad the stench that I suppose
He would have gagged had he a nose.

As he rose without a sound,
Dripping maggots on the ground,

It slowly dawned upon his brain
His wife had played the role of Cain…

…all because he caught her cheating
With his buddy Peter Keating.

He walked all night and at the dawn
Dragged his corpse across a lawn;

And through a window slowly crept
Toward a mattress where they slept.

He squeezed their toes and gently said,
"MIND IF I JOIN YOU IN BED?"

OLD DOC PICKLE

Curious is Old Doc Pickle,
Whose exams cost but a nickel.

He'll guide you to a dim lit room
(That could use a mop and broom)

Inquire where you have a pain...
And there he'll prod you with his cane.

Should you complain your throat is sore
In your mouth he'll acid pour.

Should he find you overweight,
Sutured lips will be your fate.

If you let him siphon blood
On the floor your life will flood.

So if some night you feel a chill,
Call the Doc – but write your will!

TERRIBLE TOOTSIE

Tootsie has a terrible tongue:
Decides if you'll be saved or hung.

Should that *thing* poke out at you
Your future days are but a few:

Some accident will claim your life,
By water, rope, or carving knife:

It only takes a careless word,
Said in public, or overheard.

So never in a moment blurt,
"EAT YOUR DINNER, OR NO DESSERT!"

Or say what her late Mother said,
"NO MORE CARTOONS, TIME FOR BED!"

Or, "HURRY UP, YOU'RE LATE FOR SCHOOL!"
(Said by Dad...now ripe in pool).

Her new parents have been picked:
A kindly couple...and not too strict.

FARMER BUD

Now Farmer Bud, the silent Swede,
Is keen to what his seedlings need.

Every evening he stands guard
Lest the slugs invade his yard.

Every morning, with a mallet,
He defends his pomegranate

To those who come to tour his farm,
Everyone succumbs to harm.

Says he to they, "I LOVE TO GARDEN,
AND NOW MUST ASK TO BEG YOU PARDON:

HUMAN TISSUE IS THE MEANS
I FERTILIZE MY LIMA BEANS.

AND IF MY BEETS ARE TURNING PALE
I FEED THEM BLOOD...BY THE PAIL.

EVERYTHING TASTES BETTER FRESH
WHOSE ROOTS HAVE TAPPED SOME FLESH."

My advice? If fruit you need
Do not buy from Bud the Swede!

BOSTON TONY

Take a look at Boston Tony,
He has a brow that's very bony.

You won't find Boston in a zoo,
But lurking some dank avenue,

Or often hiding in the dark
To greet a stroller in the park.

Jungle jazz is Boston's bent:
The human bod – his instrument.

All night long he'll pound a beat
Using someone's hands and feet.

Now and then he'll stop and hum,
Then once again begin to drum.

And with a head (don't be upset),
He'll shake it like a castanet.

Should he wish a horn to toot,
A femur makes a perfect flute.

To hear his rhythms of the night,
Crack the window – but douse the light!

SHAKESPEARE LEE

"TO BE OR NOT TO BE,"
The favorite words of Shakespeare Lee.

For relatives that he cared not,
He used a bodkin on the lot.

At times, he might become Othello,
And strangle some poor random fellow.

Nor would a woman call it luck
Alone at night to meet a Puck.

At bathing women he will peer
As a lascivious King Lear.

Naturally, he is a menace
To every merchant still in Venice.

But Hamlet is his favorite guy;
Uncles, the soonest ones to die.

And thus he struts upon the stage,
A proper actor for our age.

LIVERMORE JIM

Now we come to Livermore Jim,
And while not the worst of men,

You do not want to catch his heat
By calling him a card room cheat.

He's very good at playing poker:
Up his sleeves an Ace and Joker.

With such 'skills' he seldom loses.
Call him "CHEAT!" and you risk bruises!

In his pocket is a sap
To help you take a long, long nap.

Still yell, "CHEAT!" Still insist?
A razor blade will slit your wrist.

If at your table he should crash,
Excuse yourself…but leave your cash.

VINCENT VAN GORILLA

Vincent Van Gorilla knows
How to paint a blood red rose.

As a youth he was a preacher,
But his flock called him a creature.

In despair he took to drink:
Bourbon, Rye, and printer's ink.

His brain shrank up, his lips turned blue;
He forgot the things he knew.

Thus he swilled and wandered wide,
...but with a sketchbook at his side.

On a trip to Kocomo
(Why he went there I dunno).

He saw a portrait by Van Gogh;
Decided art the way to.

Thus inflamed with new vocation,
He sought out his congregation.

Though now their faces bless the Louvre
....there are those who disapprove:

In each portrait it appears,
All his subjects have no ears!

Even worse, and very weird,
All of them have disappeared.

(I heard they went to Kocomo.
Maybe so...but I dunno.)

In any case, I have to go:
I'm being painted by Van Gogh!

SKINNY DAVE

In a dump lives Skinny Dave,
Where he can laugh and misbehave.

His only pals are Gus and Gill
Buried on a nearby hill.

Though long dead they still must eat,
And so beg Dave for juicy meat.

Some time ago he dug them up,
And offered them some things to sup:

Frogs and snakes from rusty pails,
Slimy worms and shiny snails.

But from Gill, he heard this moan,
"I GOTS TO GNAW ON FLESH AND BONE."

Soon he dropped a bloody load
Into their dim and dark abode.

So pleased were they, they did a dance,
Shaking off a million ants.

"WE LOVE YOU DAVE," said Gill and Gus,
JOIN OUR GRAVE AND LIVE WITH US."

AUNTIE LIN

Be afraid of Auntie Lin
And what she does to foolish men!

A drunk who winked and pinched her tush,
Was stapled to a thorny bush.

Another gent who flashed a leer,
Now needs a straw to drink his beer.

One old geezer, no more wiser,
Lost a molar and incisor.

Worst of all an opera guy:
He once sang bass…he now sings high.

An irony, lost to none,
Kindly Kalvin is her son.

KINDLY KALVIN

Should ANYONE deserve a heaven,
It would certainly be Kalvin

...at least on thoughts based on intent,
Not on acts malevolent.

When he grows up he wants to be
A man who aids humanity.

Oh, genius brain! Oh, noble soul!
To cure the sick his only goal!

What does he charge? Not a nickel,
(Unlike his Grandpa, Old Doc Pickle).

He records each human ill,
And concocts the proper pill:

But sad to say, like as not,
They produce horrendous snot.

Once, to end his Ma's toothache,
He excised it with a garden rake.

When his sister Sally caught a fungus
He spread hot tar on her tongus.

Like I said, the kid means well,
So on results we do not dwell.

SOUR SALLY

Sour Sally has no friends:
She sent them all to dismal ends.

To a cliff she took sweet Paul:
Somehow he tripped and had a fall.

Another boy – I'll call him Bruce -
Found a dart in his caboose.

Though she loved her cousin Brice,
She still blocked her deep in ice.

I only hope, when she gets ill…
Kalvin offers her a pill.

In any case, hers not the sin:
Her genes came from Auntie Lin.

CRASH DUMMY DWAYNE

Working as a car crash dummy,
Dwayne cracked his head, split his tummy.

After years of doing this,
He cannot speak but with a hiss.

He takes his dinner through a straw,
Held by a hand that's more a paw.

Thus he slowly grew to hate
Those who drive – it was his fate.

Now he hitches all night long,
And hissing, says, "I MUST DO WRONG."

When people offer him a ride
Next to them he'll gently slide.

…then off a cliff they'll slowly glide:
Dwayne at the wheel, the other tied.

RAILROAD RUDY

That Railroad Rudy plays with trains,
Doesn't mean he has no brains.

He watches them go round and round,
Laughs and makes a 'tooting' sound.

Then he ponders through the night:
How to murder? What method right?

He thinks so hard his eyes turn red;
His thinking throws him out of bed.

It took a year, but then he knew
The awful thing that he must do.

It was the story of the week,
How some geezer mild and meek,

Was tied across a railroad track,
Before a train chugged up his back.

How did Rudy come to wrong?
Methinks he played with trains too long.

JAUNDICE JANE

When once a joyful beauty queen,
Jane encountered someone mean.

Fed a mushroom by that fellow,
Her teeth turned black; her skin turned yellow.

Afterward, her beauty gone,
(Nose deformed, earlobes long)

She traveled here, she traveled there,
Seeking mushrooms everywhere:

To Pakistan and Martinique,
Paraguay and Mozambique.

She found two that serve her well:
Skullcap and Destroying Angel.

One killed quick, the other slow,
Both on the potty made you go.

Another turned your brain to jelly;
Another made your privates smelly.

One found in a cave of bats,
Made you vote for Democrats.

Tonight she brought me Skullcap paste,
Which I – respectfully - declined to taste.

BARNEY TOOK

May I present you Barney Took?
He calls himself a gourmet cook.

When just a teen he rolled up flies
Fed to his Sis in muddy pies.

Now grown up, on your tray,
He'll plate a road kill for entree.

Should you choose an appetizer,
A stone will crack your incisor.

To top it off, for dessert,
From raw squid he'll squeeze a squirt.

His specialty is Escargot
Harvested from Kokomo:

Kept in a pail to abide
Soaking up insecticide.

BROOMSTICK MINDY

There is a witch that lives nearby
Who rides a broom across the sky.

She does the things that witches do
Casting spells, and making brew.

Her favorite potion causes itch.
Clothing? You can't wear a stitch!

She knows a spell that makes green hair
Grow on your body everywhere.

She can lengthen up your lip,
As well lop inches off your pip.

She cast that latter spell on me,
Now I sit when I have to pee.

SILENT GUS

Arriving on the midnight bus,
Came Silent Gus to visit us.

The night was cold, the sky was clear;
He lugged a gym bag full of gear:

A paring knife, a thing with wires,
A saw, an awl, a pair of pliers.

You'd think, with all these things of pain,
He would have brought some Novocaine!

He spent the night and not a word
From his closed lips was ever heard.

Now he's gone and nevermore
Will I open up the door.

SIMPLE SADIE

Oh, be afraid of Simple Sadie!
If you don't you'll be so saddie.

One day her Daddy took a nap;
And found a Spider in his lap.

When her Brother donned his pants
He found them full of Fire Ants.

In her Sister's cheese burrito
She stuffed a very large mosquito.

To Grandma Rolleen she gave a rose:
A Bee buzzed out and stung her nose.

Although some think she's very nice,
Offering lemonade with ice,

The real truth will make you blue:
She has a bug that waits for you.

FORMALDEHYDE CLYDE

As a kid, Clyde wasn't normal:
A bit too morbid; a bit too formal.

He spent his youth stuffing cats
(After smashing them with bats).

Then with care he'd make their features
Look the same as living creatures.

He became a famed mortician
Bringing death to new condition.

So said Clyde, "IT'S WHAT I DO,
ALONE AT NIGHT WITHOUT A CREW."

As his fame grew and spread,
Folks offered him their precious dead.

How did his expertise arrive?
He practiced years on those alive.

WINO WENDY

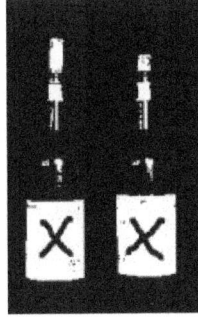

What Wendy loved was making wine.
The critics raved, "DIVINE! DIVINE!"

Some called it Zin, some Tempranillo;
"NEITHER," said one, "It's NEBBIOLO."

One claimed, "I SNIFF A BIT OF MINT,
KUMQUAT PEEL...BUT JUST A HINT...

A SCENT OF PLUM -- MAYBE PEAR --
WITH JUST A WHIFF OF UNDERWEAR."

Another said, his name was Tex,
"VERY SMOOTH, AS WELL COMPLEX."

Said a Chinese fella, who looked Danish,
"WHAT I LIKE MOST IS THE FINISH!"

Kasper Karp from Kocomo,
As to the type, said "MERLOT."

A Tunisian man with Tourette
Swore up and down it was Malbec.

She won five medals, all were gold,
And the entire vintage sold.

She told the truth, if you want to know,
From a cell in Kokomo:

The credit goes to Hubbie Clyde
And, of course, formaldehyde.

UNCLE HIRAM

Now we come to Uncle Hiram
Just escaped from the asylum.

For twenty years he screamed and raved
And not a day did he behave.

It seems two men in Doctor smocks
Gave him daily jolts and shocks.

They tucked him in a metal bed,
Strapped his feet and strapped his head.

Switched on the juice and watched him sizzle,
Cooled him down with a water drizzle.

He lost his teeth, he lost his hair,
Spittle flying everywhere.

So Uncle Hiram took an oath
That such 'care' would come to both.

It took him years (his mind was slow)
But one day he made them glow.

Now he's out upon the town
Dressed in institution brown.

A word of warning – if I might –
Don't let him catch you wearing white!

ANGELIC APRIL

If one truth I could instill:
Don't turn your back on sweet April.

You might be tempted, 'cuz her smile
Lacks the slightest hint of guile.

Some even claim they see a glow,
Above her head, a white halo.

But beware! She'll take a swipe
At your noggin with a pipe.

Then she'll grin and swing once more
As you lay twitching on the floor.

Meeting April? Just say, "HI."
Then turn around and say, "GOODBYE."

GRAMMA DOTTIE

Never let old Grandma Dottie
Plop you in a tub that's hottie.

As you slowly turn and boil
In she'll dribble olive oil.

In she'll toss rotted greens,
Pepper, salt, and lima beans.

In goes pasta, rigatoni;
Still in shell, abalone.

At the very last she'll add
A quart of milk that has gone bad.

Then she'll stir you with a spoon
Do a jig and start to croon:

"HEE, HEE, HEE," and "HO, HO, HO,
CHEW A FINGER, MUNCH A TOE!"

Soon containers she will fill
To bring to children who are ill.

CAMPGROUND DONNA

Do not mess with Campground Donna:
Meeting her you'll never wanna.

She shares a tent with Tahoe Meg,
Who has one arm….and extra leg.

They play Parcheesi, lantern low,
Until 2am – then out they go

To prowl the camp with tin snips,
Collecting certain kinds of tips.

Then back to tent in joy they goes
To make some necklaces of toes.

(They sell them at a decent price.
I purchased one, it is quite nice).

NANNY LUGOSI

Now we come to Nanny Lugosi;
A criminal whose crimes are grossi.

As a child she loved to knit
Scarves and cloaks that never fit;

And underwear (lacking flies)
Embroidered with blue butterflies.

How her parents laughed and giggled!
How their bellies jerked and jiggled!

Now bugged-eyed, with greasy pores,
Once a month she knocks on doors.

Woe to the one who lets her in
Thinking that she might be kin.

With thread and needle late the night
She sews her victim nice and tight.

Then to the newly risen moon
She presents a blue cocoon.

And, of course, she is a nanny:
Have you a child or sweet old granny?

JOSEFIEND

In a spider web she'll wait,
For a man to meet his fate.

In any case, she's very mean,
And why they call her Josefiend.

She calls her victims on the phone,
And speaking with a husky moan,

Proposes that they make a date –
Explaining that she needs a mate.

She promises she will appear
At 3 A.M., in clothing sheer.

It's sad to say how many men
Banish sense to enter sin.

Rare the male who can escape
Women wearing but a cape.

Thus their blood she'll slowly draw,
And after make another call.

JASPER JIGGLES

A funny guy is Jasper Jiggles:
His hair is white and hangs in squiggles.

He loves to play, he lives to pun;
He choked his children one by one.

To play hop-frog, on a lark,
He took his kiddies to the park.

His lips spread wide, as if to joke,
He asked them if they'd like to croak!

He laughed so hard he almost died
(Humanity would not have cried).

Now he lives in Kokomo,
A town where police will never go.

PIPSQUEAK PAULEY

Keep away from Pipsqueak Pauley,
Whose eyes are black, whose skin is paley.

His mother runs a small hotel
(Weak on service, strong on smell)

In the town of Kokomo,
(Arrive in daylight...if you go).

When a traveler goes to sleep,
Pipsqueak Pauley starts to creep.

Quietly from room to room,
He softly treads the midnight gloom.

(On those evenings sans a moon)
Collecting oddments with a spoon.

What does he prize? It's no surprise:
What he scoops out are the eyes.

WENDELL WEEMS

Have I mentioned Wendell Weems?
The man impervious to screams?

He so hates to hear complaint,
You won't confuse him with a saint.

So save your breath and do not squeal
As you get a dermal peel.

And do not make the slightest peep
If your tongue you hope to keep.

Should he hear the slightest sigh,
Weems will never let you die.

If Wendell Weems get hold of you,
Make no sound until he's through.

FRISCO PHILLY

A thoughtful man is Frisco Philly,
Master of the bat and billy.

He knows best those painful points
Nestled there between our joints.

He works the early morning shift,
2 AM…if you get my drift.

He'll ask you for your wallet nice.
If you refuse…his eyes turn ice.

But he'll repeat himself again
Ending with the words "…MY FRIEND."

Should you still hesitate or balk,
His billy club will start to talk.

A single word will turn your knee
From sturdy bone to grape jelly.

And should it need to utter verb,
You'll not have an untouched nerve.

When I met Philly, I was a talker.
Now I seldom speak and use a walker.

ANOPHELES ANN

Anopheles Ann has a stinger
Sewn in each and every finger.

One shoots cyanide in your hide,
So quickly you won't know you died.

Another, filled with Bok Choy Cider,
Makes your sphincter a lot wider.

One brings twitches, burps, and howls,
As you geyesr out your bowels.

With just one prick of chloroform
You won't miss your pip till morn.

Most stings bring death; others, coma.
In all cases, hematoma.

Expect a lot of tears and sweat;
Expect to make your undies wet.

Anopheles Ann buzzes streets,
And winks at every man she meets.

REDLIGHT LOUIE

Redlight Louie (late mental ward)
Runs over things when he gets bored:

A red stop sign, a red mail box;
A man from a deli carrying lox.

A fence or post; a cat with cane;
A Pollyanna singing in the rain.

With headlights off, he drives at night;
Never signals left or right.

Think a helmet will keep you well?
Not much better than a thin eggshell.

Safe in a crosswalk? Don't suppose!
Look both ways, don't pick your nose!

His relatives in Kokomo
Say he drives a Black Nismo.

SQUEAKS

Our cat Squeaks is very mellow
Visit her and she'll purr "HELLO."

But when the day expels the light
Squeaks presents a different sight:

Gone the aforementioned mellow:
Her ears turn down; her eyes turn yellow.

The teeth you never saw before
Hungrily now scrape the floor.

She hunts her prey when street lamps burn:
When her eyes can best discern.

Did I forget to mention that
Her prey is larger than a rat?

It has two legs, a pair of hands,
You might have guessed, upright it stands.

She'll wait in stealth behind a bush
Then sink her claws into a tush.

And though a gal may wear a coat,
It does not hide her tender throat

Again I said, Squeaks is mellow.
Should you visit, she'll purr "HELLO."

RIESLING ROZ

Never speak to Riesling Roz!
I tell you this in dread because

She sells organs on the sly:
A liver, heart, an ear or eye.

As you speak she'll tally up
Then invite you home to sup.

While you scarf down her lasagna,
With a knife she'll be upon 'ya,

Taking this and taking that,
Dissecting you upon a mat.

Yet at times she is divine
…after drinking Riesling wine.

ROLLEEN

Of blood and gore she is the queen:
May I present my wife Rolleen.

She does her mayhem by the week:
Oh, pity those asleep or weak!

Every Monday she trots out
To beat a geezer with a trout.

Every Tuesday she attacks
A Swedish tourist with an ax.

On Wednesday mornings down the stairs
Go veterans in wheelchairs.

Every Thursday, the blind she'll lead
To the zoo where lions feed.

On Friday nights, Democrats
Are slowly fed to hungry rats.

On Saturdays, bound and gagged,
Out to sea the deaf are dragged.

On Sundays, she is almost good,
Deciding only to be rude.

So should you see Rolleen stroll by
The day will tell you how you'll die.

THE TOWN

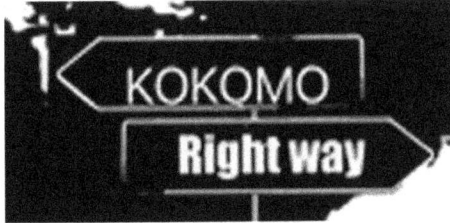

The greatest fear has no face:
It's not a person, but a place.

Woe to the traveler late at night
Who turns left instead of right.

All streets lead in, never out,
No matter how you drive about.

You cannot stop and ask for help:
No services, not even Yelp.

At sunset all the locals hide
Behind stout doors electrified.

About that time, as seasons vary,
Dead emerge from the cemetery.

They need love and seek the places
Where last they kissed their spouse's faces.

They tug on doors; they rap on glass,
Yet rarely find a way to pass.

They choke up words along with bugs,
"OPEN UP, I NEED YOUR HUGS!"

Shunned, abandoned, and denied,
They'll seek another groom or bride.

This dismal place you would know?
Read the sign...Kokomo.

THE END

www.ingramcontent.com/pod-product-compliance
Lightning Source LLC
Chambersburg PA
CBHW031334040426
42443CB00005B/346